The Pursuit of Happiness:

Ten Ways to Increase Your Happiness

By

Paul G. Brodie

The Pursuit of Happiness: Ten Ways to Increase Your Happiness

Copyright @ 2016 by Paul G. Brodie

Editing by Devin Rene Hacker

Published in the United States by BrodieEDU Publishing, 2016.

Disclaimer

The following viewpoints in this book are those of Paul Brodie. These views are based on his personal experience over the past forty years on the planet Earth, especially while living in the great state of Texas.

The intention of this book is to share his stories of both success and struggles with pursuing happiness and what has worked for *him* through this journey.

All attempts have been made to verify the information provided by this publication. Neither the author nor the publisher assumes any responsibility for errors, omissions, or contrary interpretations of the subject matter herein.

This book is for entertainment purposes only. The views expressed are those of the author alone and should not be taken as expert instruction or commands. The reader is responsible for his or her future action. This book makes no guarantees of future success. However by following the steps that are listed in this book the odds of increased happiness definitely have a much higher probability.

This book is dedicated to my mom, Barbara "Mama" Brodie. Without her support and motivation (and incredible cooking) I would literally not be here today

Table of Contents

Contact Information

Feedback

Free Audiobook Offer

Are you a fan of audiobooks? I would like to offer you the audiobook of Motivation 101 for free. All you need to do is go to my website at www.BrodieEDU.com/freeaudiobook and provide your e mail address in exchange for the free digital download. The audiobook will only be available on the website for a limited time as I offer free goodies to my readership on a regular basis.

Foreword by J. Dean Craig

"Life, Liberty, and the pursuit of Happiness." How many times have I as an American encountered this phrase? Set forth in my country's Declaration of Independence, I often take for granted how truly revolutionary that phrase is. It may surprise some of my compatriots to know that the original phrase most often heard during our country's early colonial protests was: "life, liberty, and *property*." Moreover, other countries do not share America's appreciation of this adage. Canadians cry: "peace, order, and good government." The motto of the French is: "liberty, equality, and fraternity."

With early colonists looking for property, and the French longing for brotherhood, what caused the American founders to adopt this seemingly fanciful axiom? A pursuit of *happiness*? I believe that it was their recognition of a very basic human need: a need that encompasses the end desire of all our best laid plans. Even if our attempts are misguided, or our decisions wrong, every action we take essentially is to better our, or our loved-one's, situation. Simply put: every human desires and deserves to be happy. It is in his most recent book that Paul Brodie embraces the spirit of that early revolution.

No stranger to upheavals, Paul has had his share — professional and personal. Grappling with them one by one, and learning from each, Paul has always had a way of translating his experiences to lessons for those of us that seek out his advice. I have had the benefit to tap into that resource for the last fifteen years. During that time I have known Paul, I have witnessed him grow from learner and leader in college, to manager and trainer in the professional world, on to educator and motivator in public schools. In each of his past lives I have been honored to share in his experiences.

I enjoyed studying alongside Paul in college. It was there that most of our experiments in leadership were tried: taking our failures as warnings and putting our successes to good use later in life. In the workforce, we both used the other as a sounding board for our ideas to better train and manage our staff. During his life as a teacher, Paul has invited me to speak to his classes. Paul has always taken great amusement in my tales from abroad, and as an educator it was natural that he would want to share them. It was there in the classroom that I first witnessed Paul's gift to motivate others.

Now as a motivator and speaker on campuses, Paul shares with young people across the country that gift that I have relied on for fifteen years. Whether convincing me as a less than exemplar student that I actually did have the acumen to become an attorney, or simply using the right words to nudge me to finish a forward for a new book, it has been a pleasure to receive his guidance and share in his journey.

Now in his fifth book, Paul takes his reader through his own personal journey, allowing those that follow him to relate and to be guided by his insights. At the end of each chapter readers will be pressed to answer questions relating to their own journey. Through this guided review, they will come to discover their own path to happiness. With an easy-to-read style, and honest accounts of his own experience, Paul succeeds in placing a path ahead: enabling his followers to pursue the greatest of human needs.

J. Dean Craig, Esq.
Kingsville, Texas

Introduction

Welcome to the Pursuit of Happiness. My intention with this book is to help increase your happiness. We will cover ten different ways that you can increase your happiness through a variety of techniques and concepts.

One of the biggest challenges in our lives is the ability to be happy. There is a lot of negativity that we must consistently battle throughout our lives. I will provide you with the necessary tools to improve your happiness. In 2014, I created the Pursuit of Happiness seminar with the intention of helping people shift their focus to the happier aspects of their lives.

Chapter 1 encourages you to love what you do. One of the biggest questions to ask yourself is "Do you love what you're doing in your career?"

Chapter 2 is dedicated to one of the most important parts of pursuing your happiness. You first must recognize that happiness is a choice, and then decide whether or not to make that choice to be happy.

Chapter 3 covers gratitude. I cannot emphasize how important showing gratitude daily is and how it can impact your day. We will cover five ways to express gratitude every morning.

Chapter 4 is about money and happiness. This is the longest chapter and the most emotional for me. Deeply personal stories are shared from my past to express how I've seen firsthand why happiness is much more important than money.

Chapter 5 is what life is all about. This chapter focuses on family and friendship and how it contributes to our daily happiness.

Chapter 6 is about enjoying the things that matters most. I cover the importance of having a fulfilling career and the celebrations that bring friends and family together - how it all comes full circle.

Chapter 7 is about the power of self-suggestion and how it can help you each morning.

Chapter 8 details the importance of investing in our minds. It is one of the best investments that we can make in the effort to better ourselves.

Chapter 9 addresses worrying. Worrying is an absolutely normal response, but I'll teach you strategies to keep it from consuming your mind.

Chapter 10 is dedicated to asking yourself what happiness means to you. Our closest friends and family, our extended family and even our colleagues can all be part of that happiness.

I hope that this book helps you in your journey to improve your happiness. My philosophy in anything I do in life, whether it's teaching, giving motivational seminars, and writing and coaching, is to have the power of one. The power of one is my goal to help at least one person. I hope that person is you.

Coaching Offer

Are you looking for a coach to help with turning your book into a bestseller?

Are you looking for a coach to help with weight loss, increasing your motivation, or improving your positive thinking?

Contact Paul today at Brodie@BrodieEDU.com to set up a free call.

Chapter 1 Love What You Do

"Success is not the key to happiness. Happiness is the key to success. If you love what you are doing. You will be successful." Albert Schweitzer

As we celebrated Valentine's Day 2016 with grade level parties throughout the school, I found myself reminiscing quite a bit. Typically, there is a very interesting combination of hormones and candy during Valentine's Day celebrations. This day was no different.

The difference this time was that this was the first year that I have experienced Valentine's Day at the Elementary School level, without being a student myself. My previous seven years in teaching were spent at the Junior High School and Middle School level so this experience was definitely different, but still fun.

The reason I'm bringing this holiday up is because I found true happiness in my career on Valentine's Day 2008. In my first book, Eat Less and Move More, I covered my journey into education and how February 14, 2008 would be a day that defined my life.

It was that day when I took my first substitute teaching assignment and realized that I wanted teaching to become my career. I have taught ever since and it has been one of the most rewarding career decisions that I have made.

This day also helped me to define what happiness was for me. Happiness is doing what you enjoy in life both professionally and personally. Having a career that you love makes all the difference because if you are not happy at work, then the chances of you being happy after work with family or out with friends aren't very likely.

If we are doing what we love, then it will never feel like work. Up until this past school year I always enjoyed teaching and loved working with my kids. In August 2015, I lost the love to teach. It took until January 2016 to find that happiness again.

Last July, I received a call from the Director of Special Education in my school district. She contacted me about staffing moves they were making and I was given the opportunity to start a brand new Special Education program at an elementary school. I was excited about the change. Transitioning to elementary school was a huge adjustment.

I will freely admit that I struggled during the first several weeks. Transitioning from teaching junior high to elementary was overwhelming. My classroom was significantly smaller, in fact, less than half the size of a regular classroom. I needed to find room for myself, my teacher assistant, and ten special needs students. It took a lot of patience.

That first month was the roughest, but we made it work. By the end of September we had everything on point and the classroom was becoming successful. The problem I faced was that I was no longer enjoying teaching.

Over the summer I started to write my books and had a successful launch for Eat Less and Move More. I wrote my second book, Motivation 101 that I would launch in October. I loved the time I was spending writing my books and my public speaking was doing really well.

During the fall, I decided that the school I taught at was not the best fit for me. Therefore, I decided to resign in mid-October. It was not a decision that I took lightly. A lot of time and thought went into that choice. Initially, I planned to retire from teaching and focus on my company full time.

The decision to resign was absolutely the right one. The administration was very hands on and overall it was not a good fit for me. It was not anything personal against the administration, but more the lack of resources within the room. Additionally, only having one assistant who was out of the room for a majority of the day due to an inclusion model for some students wasn't the best dynamic. Half of my kids could be violent and that room had the potential to be recipe for disaster.

By December I realized that I still had a love of teaching and that the situation was the real problem. I have always believed that we create our own environment. I decided to make my broom closet of a room the best I could to enhance the environment for the remainder of the school year.

Another bonus was that two opportunities had presented themselves in December. I was informed that the After-School program was most likely returning to my previous school in Birdville and that the Principal already wanted me to come back to run the program. The other opportunity, an opening in another district similar to my current assignment, but with less students, two teacher assistants, and a classroom that would be three times the size of said broom closet.

In life, no situation will be ideal and there will always be challenges. However, there are situations where you can see the writing on the wall and you must not be afraid to make changes. I had no regrets about resigning because I knew there was something much better on the horizon. You must believe in not only yourself, but your value. There are many jobs and careers out there, and I honestly believe that there is an ideal career out there for everyone. You just have to open your heart and your eyes to see it as opportunities will always present themselves.

Ask yourself the following questions:

Do you love what you're doing in your career?

Are you unhappy with your career?

If you are unhappy then why are you still at your current job?

Chapter 2 Happiness is a Choice

"Most folks are about as happy as they make up their minds to be." Abraham Lincoln

If you get one thing out of reading my fifth book I hope that it is that happiness is a choice. In Motivation 101, I wrote about becoming a master of your own universe. Being the master of your own universe is simple. It is the belief that you control everything in your mind and thus everything in your world. Your emotions, thoughts, and perceptions are all part of your own universe that you must master. You must believe in yourself and not rely on the validation of others. This relates to your own happiness.

You must choose whether you want to be happy. It is your choice. The only perception that matters in life is your own. You are the one who will decide to be happy.

The title of this book is The Pursuit of Happiness. We all pursue happiness. The question is will you achieve it? We will not always be happy, but we will not always be sad. It is a tough balance, but it is a choice.

In chapter one, I covered my choice to be happy in a tough situation with my classroom and lack of resources. Honestly, I spent a lot of time last fall fighting a severe case of depression.

In Positivity Attracts, I covered my battle with depression. One of my greatest personal battles in my life has been overcoming depression. Most days I would feel great, but there are days when I felt awful and questioned many things about my life. Depression is visible on both sides of my family. I have even lost family members to depression over the years. It's a big part of why I fight the battle to stay positive and motivated on a daily basis.

It is very easy for our dark side to take over. You may start to develop a negative mindset. Through that negative mindset you will start to feel like a victim. During that time you may start to believe that there is always something bad about to happen.

My cousin, Anya lost her battle against depression several years ago. She had fought depression and mental illness for most of her life. Sadly, she committed suicide by jumping out of a 12th floor window of a hospital where she was being treated. The news shocked my entire family. We knew that she had depression, but we never realized how bad it became. It was a very sad time for our family and it made us all really think about life.

My father also fights depression and is on daily medication to help with the battle. He is a former alcoholic who fortunately turned his life around fifteen years ago. Now he's in much better shape. My grandfather fought depression too. He ended up dying in his fifties due to his declining health that was partly attributed to him fighting depression.

Depression is a deeply personal thing to cover, but I feel it is necessary when becoming our greatest champion and pursuing our own happiness.

Happiness is a choice that you must train your mind to make. In this book, I will share how I have trained my mind to pursue happiness.

Ask yourself the following questions:

Would you prefer to be happy, sad, or angry?

Do members of your family suffer from depression?

Have you fought depression?

Have you lost family members to depression?

Chapter 3 Expressing Gratitude

"Gratitude bestows reverence, allowing us to encounter everyday epiphanies, those transcendent moments of awe that change forever how we experience life and the world." John Milton

One of the most important things that I have learned over the past several years is to express gratitude. Every morning I think of five things that I am grateful for.

This is my gratitude list

1. My family having good health
2. My friends
3. My home
4. My career
5. My choice to be happy every morning

Every time that I think of my gratitude list it makes me happy because my family had good health for the most part, my friends are amazing and happy, I am blessed to have a dream home, I love being a teacher, and I get to drive my dream car daily.

It is amazing the difference when you focus on what you have, versus what you don't. I feel our society always wants to focus on what is missing.

Why don't we focus on what we have in life? Good health, family, friends, and a home and transportation. Those are some pretty awesome things to be grateful for.

I have found that my happiness significantly increases by focusing on what I am grateful for first. There will always be areas of opportunity for improving our lives, but the main takeaway is to focus on what we have versus what we don't have.

Television shows are something we all use for escapism. Some love watching the Real Housewives of Atlanta (or one other of the numerous cities). My mom is a fan of The Bachelor and The Bachelorette. My dad likes the world series of poker. My escapism includes Pro Wrestling and UFC. I have an amazing group of fellow educators who are wrestling fans as well. We call our group the Four Horsemen in tribute to Ric Flair and his group. With WrestleMania being in my hometown of Arlington this year, we are going to be attending the event. We will be enjoying a day of escapism to celebrate our love for sports entertainment.

Wrestling tends to have a stigma because it's pre-determined, but the damage wrestlers incur through high risk moves and crazy stunts in combination with a hectic travel schedule, is real. Many wrestlers die young and quite a few have their careers ended early due to damage they have incurred in the ring.

Bryan Danielson, otherwise known as Daniel Bryan is considered by many to be the best technical wrestler in the world for many years. He retired on Monday, February 8, during the final segment of the Monday Night RAW television show. During his speech he talked about the multiple concussions that he has endured and due to those concussions and seizures he needed to retire.

Bryan could have been angry and bitter about having to retire because of the injuries he has suffered. Instead, he spent his speech expressing gratitude for his career.

"I am grateful because wrestling doesn't owe me or anybody back there, it doesn't owe us anything. WWE doesn't owe us anything. You guys don't owe us anything. We do this because we love to do this." Bryan Danielson

His speech was over twenty minutes and Bryan chose to show gratitude for what he has received over the years. He was not angry or bitter; instead he focused on all of the opportunities he was able to take advantage of.

"I am grateful because I get to come out here in front of what I feel is my hometown fans. I get to announce my retirement in front of a bunch of people who love me, that special moment I had with my dad, I get to share this moment with my mom, with my sister, with my family, with my friends. I get to share that with them. I get to share it with you. I get to share it with my wife in the back. I get to share it and with all these wonderful human beings that I have spent the last 15 years of my life with. I am grateful" Bryan Danielson

He concluded his speech in an epic fashion by having the entire arena chant the word, YES.

"Now tomorrow morning, I start a new life, a life where I'm no longer a wrestler. But that is tomorrow and that is not tonight. I have one more night to feel this energy and feel this crowd, so if I could just get one last 'Yes' chant, I would really appreciate it." Bryan Danielson

Ask yourself the following questions:

What are you grateful for?

What five things are you grateful for each morning?

What does negativity do compared to gratitude?

Chapter 4 Money and Happiness

"If you weren't happy yesterday, you won't be happy tomorrow. It's money. It's not happiness." Marc Cuban

While creating the outline for this book, I knew this would be the chapter that I would have the most difficulty writing due to emotions from the past and what I needed to share with you, the reader. There was a lot that happened with my parents and there was a period of time in my teenage years when both my mom and I, were by definition, homeless. We had a place to stay, but it was not our own.

In this chapter, I am going to reflect back to my early years in life. I will be focusing on times in my life that were both happy and sad, as well as the impact that money (or lack thereof) had on it. One thing that I want to make clear is that I hold no ill will towards those who caused me pain in my earlier years. I believe in the power of forgiveness. While some of those feelings may never be forgotten, they have been forgiven.

This chapter does not exactly portray my dad in the best light, and he will be the first to admit that he has a lot of regrets about the past, along with all of the mistakes that he made. My current relationship with my dad is the best it has ever been and it has taken a long time to get to this point. My youth was not an easy time, but it showed me early on that you do not need to have a lot of money to be happy.

When I was growing up, I was raised in a beautiful neighborhood called Interlochen in North Arlington. It was a very affluent neighborhood. We moved there when I was five years old. Both of my parents were executives for Combined Insurance and they were very successful with setting insurance sales records and were rising through the ranks at the executive level.

The 80's were a pretty wild time and my dad was particularly skilled in the areas of excessive drinking and womanizing. As I got older, things got worse. My dad had a huge falling out with his company and ended up quitting when I was just eight years old. I was never very close with my dad in my earlier years and in those days I was quite frankly happier when he was away on business. He could be very mean to both my mom and I when he was drinking.

My mom on the other hand, was the rock of the family and I hated when she was away on business. Growing up I had several nannies that helped take care of me since both of my parents were away on business most weekdays. My first two nannies were wonderful, but the third one was very mean and I could not stand her. It was not that she was strict, my other nannies were also strict, but they were still fair. Her problem was that she was very mean spirited and selfish. I did not get along with her.

After quitting Combined Insurance, my dad formed a new insurance company called Brodie International. My mom also chose to quit Combined and join his company. He attempted to raid Combined and recruited several of their top sales people to work with him.

The company had limited success. My dad wasted a lot of money leasing a fancy office in Dallas and buying extravagant items for his office, rather than actually running the business and investing properly in the infrastructure. He mismanaged the company and it did not work out. After a year, he shut down the company and became an independent insurance sales person with another insurance company. My mom did the same.

Money was tight. My dad went through all of the family savings. I was much happier though because my mom was at home a little more and my dad continued to travel. By the time I was ten, things got really bad between my parents. They were arguing constantly and my dad was continuously picking fights with my mom. There were even times when he would hit or kick my mom, which he made a point to do it in front of me.

During this time my weight was starting to get out of control. The third nanny did not care what I ate because she was too lazy to cook anything. My previous nannies always made sure that I ate healthy. My mom always made sure there was plenty of food in the house so they could cook a healthy dinner for me. This third nanny could not care less and tended to rely on bringing in fast food for dinner.

With my weight getting out of control, my dad didn't really want to spend time with me. He was very critical of my weight gain and would even call me names in regards to my weight at times. My dad wanted a fit and macho son that he could hang out with and be proud of. I apparently was not that person. He took it out on me by playing mean jokes on me and even threw both me and my bike in the swimming pool on several occasions while I was fully dressed. He thought it would be funny for him and his drinking buddies as he always wanted to entertain not only himself, but his friends too.

Things came to a head in January 1986 when he split with my mom and moved out. He packed his things and even took all of the furniture out of the guest bedroom. At the time, I was in the Texas boys' choir and had choir rehearsal on Monday nights after school. My dad picked me up from the bus stop one night in January 1986 and brought me home. As we went inside, I saw that furniture was missing. I asked him what was going on and he told me that he was moving out. He then said he had to go and gave me twenty dollars. He told me to tell my mom that he moved out and just like that he left.

My mom arrived about an hour later. She was working locally, but was running late that night. As a ten year old child, I then had to explain why the furniture was missing and that her husband had moved out. This actually made me very happy because my dad, who's abusive and mean tendencies were escalating, had finally left. I knew that we would probably end up losing the house, but I was happy about it. I no longer had to worry about my dad finding ways to mess with me or hurt my mom. I was finally free of his hatred.

It was not an easy conversation to have with my mom, but I told her what happened. I immediately gave her the twenty dollars that my dad gave me as I knew she would need the money. She was heartbroken and cried. It was definitely a night I will never forget.

We ended up having to sell the house and moved out in July 1987. Those nineteen months were a very happy time. There were times where we had very little food, but mom was working for a health club and eventually became a manager at the club. It was stressful at times, but at least we didn't have to worry about my dad.

After leaving my childhood home, we briefly moved to a house that could be more accurately described as a shack, in Ft Worth for a few weeks. After that, we moved to a townhouse in Arlington because it was still in the zone for my school. Choosing to stay in the same area though probably was not the best move.

In Positivity Attracts and Motivation 101, I wrote about my experiences with bullying. I talked about getting bullied daily and this was the time period when it was the worst.

Part of the reason I was targeted had to deal with the fact that I was no longer living in the nice house in Interlochen. A few students in particular were very happy about it because they lived near me in the same complex where we had the townhouse. Half the students were middle and upper middle class and the others were considered poor, and on free or reduced lunch at school. Due to what happened with my parents and our lack of money, I entered the free lunch program. The students who once viewed me as a wealthy kid now saw that I was living in their neighborhood. This made them very happy about my situation because they no longer had a reason to feel any jealously towards me. They would constantly knock on the door and run away. Other times they would knock on the door and want me to go outside to fight them. In contrast, the middle class and upper middle class kids no longer wanted me to hang out with them because I was now considered a poor kid to them. To this day it still amazes me how kids could act that way. It gave me a new perspective on how silly it was to view others by how much money their family had or for the size of their homes. It was not always a happy time, but I was still glad to be away from my dad who at this point was getting remarried to his third wife.

We did not have much money, but I was still relatively happy. By January 1988, things were getting worse at school. After one particularly brutal day, I was covered in bruises. By that point the teachers who tended to look the other way, were completely ignoring what was happening. This also happened to be my final day at Pope. All of the students were walking laps outside on this huge field for PE. The ringleader of most of my previous beatings decided to directly walk across the field with five of his buddies. The PE teacher did nothing… I still remember Stephen coming up to me and telling me, "This is five verses one, and much better than two verses one."

In November 1987, this ringleader wanted to fight me one on one in the classroom. The moment the teacher left, I went to her desk to turn in my classwork. Stephen started to call me names and wanted to fight me. I told him I didn't want to fight.

He charged right at me anyway. Previously, I had taken some karate and by instinct put my right hand out as an open hand palm thrust. I did not want to hit him, but I also needed to defend myself. My hope was that it would push him away, and it certainly did.

Somehow he ran right into my hand which busted up his nose pretty badly. He was covered in blood and was holding his face when the teacher finally returned a few minutes later. That's right; the teacher not only left the classroom with no coverage, but was also gone for several minutes. She left a "student leader" in charge of the classroom who happened to be a friend of Stephen's.

The best part was that other students told the teacher that Stephen started it and that the student leader let it happen. The teacher asked Stephen if he was alright and he said that he needed to go to the bathroom. I found out later that day that he was crying in the bathroom for a good twenty minutes. He was also apparently telling another student in the bathroom how he was going to make me suffer and gang up on me with his friends.

Stephen kept his word. Each day after that was difficult. That infamous day in January was the final straw for my mom. She picked me up at 5 pm on that Friday at school. Mom was late because she told me that she found us a house to rent in South Arlington and she was getting me out of that school.

We went straight to the office at school and she told the secretary that she was withdrawing me from Pope. The secretary told her that mom could not move and mom responded that we were leaving regardless. Mom got me out of Pope and we were on a new journey. I felt free.

As usual there were several kids waiting for me across the street to fight me. We walked right past them and went to the car. One of the kids yelled out asking me where I was going. My mom responded by calling the group hooligans and that I would no longer be at Pope to be bullied.

After moving and getting settled in to our new home on the following Monday, my mom went back to Pope to get all of my items out of my locker. What happened next would be the talk of the school for several weeks... Mom got all of my things and proceeded to chew out the 6th grade teachers for not doing anything about the bullying throughout the school year. She then went to the principal's office and told the principal to take control back of his school as no one should have gone through the abuse that I had put up with.

In hindsight, it was that year that eventually would draw me into education. I could never stand by and do nothing like those teachers did. What I realized was there was a lot of dysfunction in education and they needed teachers that would not tolerate bullying. As a teacher, I have always protected my kids and I swore that no student would go through what I had to endure.

In 1988 things were going well. I liked my new school and loved the house that we were renting. It had a pool and slide and enough room for mom, myself and our two cats and two dogs. The neighborhood was really nice and things were going well, until summer.

During the summer my mom lost her job. She was working for a telemarketing company at the time. However, there was a shakeup and she was let go. This was quite the curveball and mom was not able to find another job for a while.

We had no income and by the end December we had to move out. Instead of celebrating the holidays properly, we were trying to figure out what to do next. A family friend told mom there was a family who was looking for someone to help take care of their kids, help with the cooking and cleaning of the house. Mom swallowed her pride and we went to meet the family.

She took the job. At least we had a place to stay for a few months. It was not a very happy time because the family was strange. It was a rough time, but luckily mom did find a job in April doing marketing research at the Parks Mall in South Arlington. We were able to move out and get an apartment. I loved the new apartment as we finally had a place of own again. I never cared about how big or small the home was, as long as it was our own.

Mom was doing really well in her new job. She was one of those people who had a clipboard in the mall and asked customers to do a survey about a new or existing product. She had a lot of success and quickly got promoted to assistant manager. During this time, her car broke down and the engine needed replaced. She could not afford to replace it, so we went without a car for the next five years. On the bright side, she no longer had a car payment and everything was relatively close.

Again, happiness is a choice. You can find happiness in many tough situations.

In the fall of 1989, mom found a townhouse complex that was closer to the mall and had more room. We still did not have much money, but mom was able to afford food and rent. Mom worked fifty hours a week, and walked a mile each way to work. She still found time to take care of the house and me and the animals. I will never forget the sacrifices that my mom has made for me.

I wanted to share this story because life is not easy, but money does not buy happiness. As I mentioned in Chapter 2, happiness is a choice. I've had a lot of things going on in my life and I still chose to be happy, to look at the positive side. Even when I was getting beaten up on a daily basis, I knew that we would be out of that school eventually.

In Positivity Attracts, I dedicated a chapter to forgiveness. I forgave all of those kids who bullied me. One of the kids even apologized to me when I ran into him in a movie theater in my early twenties.

In 1992, I had the opportunity to work at the same marketing research company through my mom's boss who was looking for new staff. I worked at the company for the next 13 years and was promoted multiple times. By 2001, I was the assistant manager and my mom was the branch manager. The part that I was the proudest of was that my mom never hired me or gave me any promotions. All of the promotions were through her bosses. She was very tough on me and for that I am very grateful.

From 1994 to 2005 I worked my way through college. It was a tough grind, but ten years later I finally graduated. I did end up having to take one more class in 2005, but for the most part my work was done. During New Year's Eve 2004 I told my mom how much I really appreciated all that she has done for me over the years and that I had a plan. Within two months we would get a house and that within a few years I would be able to take care of the bills so that she would be able to retire.

On February 1, 2005, we moved in to the dream home that we still have today. We were able to find the perfect home. The price was very fair and with our two incomes, we were already approved for the financing. Mom was getting close to retirement and I did not want her living in a town house because she always dreamed of having her own home again. I knew that I could make it happen.

Money does not buy happiness in my view, but if used correctly can enhance your life. I knew that I would be making more money after graduation and as my income would rise my mom's income would decrease.

Another curveball was that the market research company that we worked at was being sold. We met with the president of the company and he was straight forward about the sale. He had another position for my mom, but he would not have a local position for me. In this situation some people might get angry or bitter, instead I thanked him for that entire experience and explained that I appreciated the opportunity to work for him. At that point, I shook his hand to express my gratitude and thanked him for having a position available for my mom.

During this time I wanted to start a mediation company. I had gone through several trainings and was certified to do mediations. Unfortunately, most of the business was given to attorneys at law firms and it was going to be a tough road ahead to have a sustainable full time career in mediation.

In August 2015, I started my journey at Enterprise rent-a-car. I stayed with the company until 2007 and then went into nurse recruiting before finally taking the leap of faith and started my teaching career, where I have remained ever since.

During that timeframe my mom left market research and returned to selling insurance. Ironically she went back to Combined Insurance and worked there for several years before finally retiring in 2011. With teaching I was able to take care of the bills and my projections worked out very well. I also started BrodieEDU in 2010 and was already generating revenue through creating an after school program for low cost housing in Kentucky.

My income was in good shape and I was able to have the honor of taking care of family that took such great care of me over the years. I know that not everyone would or could do that for their family. Everyone's situation is different and at times those decisions are due to money. I am very proud to be in a situation where I have the opportunity to support my family and to also pursue my happiness as both a teacher and author.

Ask yourself the following questions:

Have you dealt with bullying in your life and did it affect your happiness?

Were you happier when you had money or when you had no money?

Do you need a lot of money to be happy?

Chapter 5 What Life is About

"Whenever I get gloomy with the state of the world, I think about the arrivals gate at Heathrow Airport. General opinion's starting to make out that we live in a world of hatred and greed, but I don't see that. It seems to be that love is everywhere. Often, it's not particularly dignified or newsworthy, but it's always there – fathers and sons, mothers and daughters, husbands and wives, boyfriends, girlfriends, old friends. When the planes hit the Twin Towers, as far as I know, none of the phone calls from the people on board were messages of hate or revenge – they were all messages of love. If you look for it, I've got a sneaky feeling you'll find that love actually is all around." Prime Minister (Hugh Grant's Character) in Love Actually

One of my favorite movies is Love Actually. In my previous books I talk about music extensively and having a song for every occasion. With music, my emergency song is We Will Rock You by Queen and Love Actually is my emergency movie. The emergency song as I covered in Positivity Attracts and Motivation 101, is for when you are having the worst possible day and it is the one song that can help you get through almost any situation.

Love Actually is my emergency movie as of 2013 because this movie helps me when I have a horrible day and need something to help fight the depression. The movie is one of my favorite movies to watch during the holiday season and any other time of the year. The first and final scenes in the movie revolve around the airport.

The quote mentioned above is what inspired me to test this theory out in 2014 as I was picking up my dad and his wife from the airport. It was at international terminal D at DFW airport. The airport is considered one of the largest and busiest in the world and as usual some flights were delayed. I ended up spending almost an hour at the terminal and observing exactly the same thing the Prime Minister refers to in the movie.

For that hour in terminal D, I saw hundreds of family and friends greeting each other. I saw nothing but love and happiness with people who were reunited after not seeing each other for days, weeks, months, and even years. Flights were arriving from all over the world and there was one recurring theme. The theme of friendship, love, and family.

The relationship with my dad by this time was much better. He had a health scare in the last 1990's which motivated him to give up drinking alcohol and quit smoking. At one point, he was smoking two packs of cigarettes a day and drinking enough whisky to keep Jack Daniels in business for life.

With the theme of friendship, love and family, it reminded me of all of the people that I love and matter most to me. My best friend, J, who very kindly wrote the foreword for this book talked a little bit about his journey in life. He lived in Thailand for two years while working for the Peace Corps. He couldn't have been happier eating sticky rice (his direct quote) and learning about new cultures. During that time he went against his hatred toward technology (again his direct quote) so that he could keep in touch with his family and me.

During that time, I was at Enterprise and wanted to get his advice about a potential career move. With the time difference of 14 hours, it was a challenge to find the right time to chat. We always made it work. One of the great things about close friends and family is that it doesn't matter how long it has been since you have seen or talked with them, it feels like yesterday. You pick right back up where you left off, like you are continuing a conversation. It was the same when J returned from the Peace Corps and we were able to hang out for the first time in over two years. The same thing happened when J went to law school and got his degree in San Antonio. Even though we had different paths in life, we still remained in contact. J will be my best friend for many years down the road.

To me, life is about enjoying the company of those that matter most to you. It does not matter where they are in the world or how long it has been since you have seen them. Friends and family are always there for you no matter the location. That to me, is what life is about in order to pursue your happiness.

Ask yourself the following questions:

Have you ever noticed how friends and family interact at the international arrivals gate?

Do you have a family member or friend who you haven't seen in a while?

How do you feel about your family and friends?

Chapter 6 Enjoy What Matters Most

"If you just focus on the work, and you don't let (those) people sidetrack you, someday when you get where you're going, you'll look around and you'll know that it was you and the people who love you that put you there and that will be the greatest feeling in the world." Taylor Swift acceptance speech for Album of the Year at the 2016 Grammy awards

Over the past eight years, for the most part I have loved teaching. The best part of the work is helping my students succeed and working with their parents to be partners in their children's educations.

Most of the parents that I have worked with have been great. Then there are parents that view school as free babysitting for their kids and just want to drop off their kid and get them after school. No questions asked. That is a universal truth in education and it is what it is. I choose to focus on the positives since there are a lot of good experiences within education.

I truly do love teaching. This is why I changed my mind about retiring and will continue my career in education. There are already offers available for me to pursue at the end of the school year. I am really excited about either staying in special education or moving to another area. The best part is having the freedom to make that choice and not be forced into staying at a place where I no longer want to be.

Teaching is great because you have a contract that lasts for a year and you can always pursue another position in another school or another district at the end of your contract. Schools are always looking for good teachers, especially in special education. Having the freedom to move schools is a privilege. Not all situations are going to be great and you must make every effort to enjoy what you are doing in life.

With family and friends, birthdays and holidays are typically the best times to get everyone together. As someone who is fortunate to have friends across the world, it is tough to get everyone together, but I still try to get as many together as possible. Every June I have a big birthday celebration with the people I care about. Then, on the third Saturday of December, we have a family Christmas Bash. During the parties it is always great to reconnect with everyone. Last year's party was one for the record book.

In December 2015, I ended up inviting my dad to the annual Christmas Party. We had been getting along really well during the past several years and I did not like the idea of him not having an opportunity to celebrate during the holidays.

We still had the occasional battle, but for the most part got on well. He has mellowed out a lot and you could clearly see that he felt very guilty about what he had done over the years to both me and my mom.

Earlier in the year he had separated from his fourth wife. I honestly believe that she is a saint for putting up with my dad for almost twenty years. I have made that very clear to her and my dad because I think she is a great person. I will admit that it felt strange having my dad at the party.

The only other party he attended was my graduation party when I got my bachelor's degree from UT Arlington. Another surprise was my second nanny, Lesley, came to the party. My dad called her and invited her to attend. It was a great surprise. I hadn't seen her in years!

My dad arrived a few minutes later and was very quiet, but friendly. I will freely admit that I felt a little weird having him at the house. Lesley asked me if I was alright as I went a little quiet after he arrived. I assured her that I was fine.

I continued to play host and introduced my dad to everyone at the party. He was very quiet during the party, but helped mom out several times with trash when it got full and moving around furniture here and there.

This was the first time that my mom and dad, Lesley and I were all together in the same place since those Interlochen days. As I played host, my dad spent over an hour with Lesley and her husband. Later in the evening, Lesley told me how proud my dad was of me for getting my bachelors and master's degrees, teaching and writing my books. She told me how happy it made her especially with how mean he was to me when I was growing up.

It was definitely strange to be told how proud he was of me, seeing as I have never heard it directly from him, but it was still good to hear. Things came full circle that night as my family, close friends, home, and career were all connected.

I wanted to share that story because what matters most to me is spending time with friends and family. One of the most important things in life is to enjoy what matters most to you. I cannot think of anything better than getting family and friends together to enjoy each other's company. Sometimes you have to look outside your own close circle and bring in your family members who you might not have had the best of relationships with. Family no matter what is family. You cannot choose your family but you can choose how you treat your family

I could have held grudges and being very vindictive towards my dad. There was a lot of anger over the years but I choose to forgive and move on. One of the great lessons I have learned in life is how much better when you let go of the past and choose to forgive and move on.

With my dad I chose to get to know him over the last decade. It was scary how similar we are at times as we have similar competitive personalities and both are former soccer players. Fortunately I also have my mom's logic, social and academic intelligence, and genuine care towards others.

Ask yourself the following questions:

What matters the most to you in life?

Do you hold a grudge or have anger towards someone in your family?

Do you have a member of your family that you have had to forgive?

Chapter 7 Power of Self-Suggestion

"Self-suggestion makes you master of yourself." W. *Clement Stone*

The power of self-suggestion is a prevailing one. I believe that you can train your mind to focus on the positive and to help with pursuing your happiness.

In chapter 3, I talked about coming up with five things that you are grateful for each morning. After you choose those five things, I suggest training your mind even further. Training your mind is just like strengthening a muscle and must be done consistently.

In Motivation 101, I wrote about starting your day on the right note as there are times that you must fight negative thoughts when you first wake up in the morning. Being positive in the morning makes all the difference in your continued journey for personal motivation. I believe that the most important part of our day is the first hour that we are awake.

On school days, I typically wake around 6:00 am. Since I usually get to bed around 11:00 pm, I am typically running on seven hours of sleep during the week. The first thing I do is take my thyroid pill, (my first book Eat Less and Move More explains why I am on a thyroid pill). I then grab my iPhone, and refer to a list I have saved of my morning motivations. Reading this helps me to get my mind centered and feeling positive to start the day. This morning motivation list is updated at least two to three times per month so that I am constantly adding things to motivate myself.

The list includes statements to get me focused such as:

What will happen in life will happen because my direction in life is already set.

Keep calm and let karma finish it.

I am going to win.

The only thing that matters is **YOUR** perception of **YOUR** life. No one else's opinion of you matters.

YOUR opinion is what is relevant in **YOUR** life.

You are the **MASTER** of your own **UNIVERSE**. Focus on how great your life is versus what you don't have.

The list especially helps if I wake up feeling negative or if I had a nightmare. One of the worst feelings is waking up from a nightmare. I only have one fear in life and that is failure. Over the years, I have learned to master most of my dreams. I can usually realize mid dream that it isn't real and that I can control the dream from that point. For the times that I do not, the list really helps.

As you can see, I make every effort to train my mind in the mornings and set the tone for the day ahead. This is where self-suggestion is critical. As a teacher, I know that I must be on point and ready to take on the day. The power of self-suggestion definitely helps to start the day on the right note.

Ask yourself the following questions:

What is the first thing you do when you wake up?

Do you typically feel positive or negative when you wake up?

Do you have a list of items to read to start your day?

Chapter 8 Invest In Your Mind

"Investing in yourself is the best investment you will ever make. It will not only improve your life, it will improve the lives of all those around you." Robin S. Sharma

One of the greatest investments that we can make is in ourselves. Investing in your mind, in my point of view, not only makes us more marketable for business opportunities, but especially helps in our growth as people.

It took me ten years of hard work to finish my bachelor's degree, but I would not have done it any other way. I was able to pay off my degree in full and have zero debt from student loans. When I got my degree I was thrilled because I was no longer committed to going to school ever again. Funny how things change.

In Eat Less and Move More, I wrote about an amazing opportunity that became available during my first year of teaching. During the spring 2009 semester, I was presented with an amazing opportunity. What I have learned in life is that when great opportunities come along, you must take them. The alternative certification program that I completed during summer 2008 had a partnership with Louisiana College in Pineville, Louisiana. The partnership was just starting and was open to all alumni of the teaching certification program. We were offered the opportunity to get our Master of Arts in Teaching within two years and would also receive eighteen hours of credit through our certification and teacher experience from our role in the classroom. It would only cost $5000.00 for grad school due to the program being brand new. I knew this was an amazing opportunity and I entered the program in the spring of 2009. This was done in addition to being a first year teacher, but I knew that I would be better because of it.

It was a challenge to say the least, but it was a great investment in my mind. I learned a tremendous amount about teaching in the classroom and it helped my growth as an educator. When opportunities present themselves, I highly recommend that you just take that leap.

There are many great opportunities not only related to getting degrees, but with resources such as Udemy courses. They have many courses online that do not cost a lot of money and can help in many areas anywhere from how to start a business, to self-help courses. Certifications are plentiful too and offer great ways to add to your toolbox of skills. Books are great resources, and also self-help websites online. There are plenty of opportunities to invest in your mind. I hope you consider taking advantage of the opportunities that are available.

Ask yourself the following questions:

How will you invest in your mind?

Are you interested in getting a degree or a second degree?

What will you get out of investing in your mind?

Chapter 9 Don't Worry

"When I look back on all these worries, I remember the story of the old man who said on his deathbed that he had a lot of trouble in his life, most of which never happened." Winston Churchill

Worrying is one of the biggest enemies against pursuing your happiness.

Worrying can include pressure at work, worrying about job security, paying the bills and trying to get rid of debt can all cause pressure. At the end of the day, worrying does not help and can actually make things worse.

One of the four truths that I cover in Positivity Attracts is: <u>The Fourth Truth:</u> *There is no point in worrying as most things never happen.*

This truth connects to the third, which is that everything happens for a reason. There is a strong underlying connection to our views on faith and the universe. I believe that our lives all have a direction. Throughout that life we are all here to learn and to endure tests and challenges. Life is a series of tests. How we react and perform to those tests are what define who we are.

I stopped worrying several years ago. At times, some of those worries make an appearance. I still bear in mind that what will happen, will happen. Every person in our lives is there for a reason, as are we in theirs.

The only thing that worrying does is make you sick both mentally and physically due to the stress it creates. Stress is the worst thing for our health. It is the cause of unhappiness and negativity for many people and can lead to numerous health issues that can eventually cause death. There is no point to worrying. Strive to be the best person that you can be on a daily basis.

Ask yourself the following questions:

Do you worry?

What do you worry about?

What can you do to worry less?

Chapter 10 What Is Happiness for You?

"Very little is needed to make a happy life; it is all within yourself, in your way of thinking." Marcus Aurelius

The title of this chapter is one of the most challenging questions that you will ever receive. What is happiness for you?

What are the things in life that make you truly happy? Is it friends and family? Is it a rewarding career? Is it traveling the world?

Happiness to me is spending time with my friends and family, having a rewarding career with teaching, and being an author and speaker.

We will not always be happy in life, but we will also not always be sad.

Happiness is also memories that I have had in past jobs with friends and remembering those good times. In early February I had training in Fort Worth for school. It was in the regional 11 headquarters and was in the area where my old Enterprise branch used to be. During the lunch break, I decided to drive past my old branch and saw that it was no longer there. The location actually moved about a mile down the street.

After driving for a few minutes I went to the farmers market where I used to get lunch at. They have a great barbecue restaurant in the market and it was great to relive those memories.

Happiness as stated multiple times in the book is a choice. Why would you focus your time and happiness on those in life that you do not like? Focus on those who care about you and ignore those who are negative. It's similar to trying to get someone to change their political views about a candidate when you know there is no way the other person will change their mind.

Another aspect of my own happiness is solitude. During the day I am around fifty teachers, my own students throughout the day, and the other 670 students that are on my campus. By the end of the day, I have had all of the socialization that I have needed and as someone who is as much as an introvert as an extravert, I like my solitude. Whether that is by enjoying my lunch in my classroom or reading a book at home, I enjoy spending time by myself.

One of my favorite times of the year is during summer. As a teacher, I am typically off from early June until mid-August. This is the time where I will take my mom on our annual family vacation, celebrate my birthday in June, workout, and enjoy the pool.

I will typically spend an hour a day by myself floating in my pool, while listening to music and reading. This time of solitude is my favorite time of the day. There is nothing better than relaxing in the pool, especially in the Texas heat.

This is also the time where I get many great ideas for my books and seminars. My iPhone is always close by so that I can write in ideas into my notes. You must love yourself and be willing to spend time on your own. If you do not love yourself then you will find it very difficult to love and care about others.

As Marcus Aurelius once said to make a happy life; it is all within you. I feel that we are the master of our own universe and we have the power to decide how happy we want to be.

One of my favorite things to do when traveling is to explore the new city. I was at a leadership conference in Las Vegas a couple of years ago and it was the first time that I had been to Vegas in many years. I was really excited about the trip and was looking forward to exploring all that was new on the Las Vegas Strip.

On the Saturday night of the conference I was looking forward to checking out the center of the strip. This had always been my favorite area. Originally, I was planning to go with a few friends from the conference, but they were still figuring out their plans. Instead of waiting around, I decided to go by myself and check out the area. I had a great time doing so. While I enjoy the company of others, I also enjoy my own company just the same.

Some people need others to be around, but to me happiness is spending time with yourself at times too. If we do not like ourselves, then it is much tougher to like other people and for them to like you.

Another aspect of happiness is how you handle jealousy. If you are jealous of others and are envious of other people's success, then it will be tough to be happy. While I am a competitive person I am not in competition with anyone, but the person I was yesterday. My goal is to be happy for other people's success. I have a lot of friends that are authors and each of them has had varying degrees of success. Some have barely made any money as an author and others have made hundreds of thousands of dollars. We are all at different points in our careers, and are not in direct competition with each other.

What I have realized is that I am where I need to be in life. I have also recognized is that I am much happier focusing on my own success and not on the success of others. If others did the same thing, I feel we would have a lot less jealously and envy in the world. It would be a happier place to live.

Ask yourself the following questions:

What is happiness to you?

Have you dealt with jealousy before?

How do you feel if others are more successful than you?

Conclusion

Through the past ten chapters we have covered a range of topics from choosing happiness and expressing gratitude to investing in your mind. In addition, we also covered a very emotional chapter about money and happiness. My hope is that this book can help with your own personal quest to increase your happiness.

I want to thank you for reading my fifth book. Writing each book is a labor of love. I write about things I am passionate about and I believe having a happy, positive and motivated mindset is one of the most important things in life.

Stayed tuned for the release of my next book, PMA: Positive Mental Attitude and I invite you to check out Eat Less and Move More, Motivation 101, Positivity Attracts, and Book Publishing for Beginners.

I would like to offer you the opportunity to read the first chapter of my next book, PMA: Positive Mental Attitude.

Go to www.BrodieEDU.com/Guide to read the first chapter.

More Books by Paul

"Quick and inexpensive reads for self-improvement, a healthier lifestyle, and book publishing"

Three time Amazon bestselling author, Paul Brodie believes that books should be inexpensive, straightforward, direct, and not have a bunch of fluff.

Each of his books were created to solve problems including living a healthy lifestyle, increasing motivation, improving positive thinking, and how to help authors publish and market their books.

What makes Paul's books different is his ability to explain complex ideas and strategies in a simple, accessible way that you can implement immediately.

Want to know more?

Go to www.BrodieEDU.com/Books

Author Resource Guide

Do you want to publish your first book?

Are you an author who is looking to grow your business and increase revenue?

In my fourth book, Book Publishing for Beginners, I offered a free guide that includes step-by-step instructions to help with recording your audiobook, how to upload your Kindle book to Amazon, and how to convert your Kindle eBook to paperback. I also provide examples of sales copy to help with book sales, how to use HTML in your book description, and how to utilize different back end products to offer your readership.

In addition, the guide includes contact information for my own personal editor and my book designer who can create a great book cover for as low as ten dollars. The first chapter of my next publishing book, Book Publishing for Authors is also offered in the guide.

I want to offer this free guide to assist in your journey of writing and publishing your own book. It is highly recommended that you also check out my Book Publishing for Beginners book as it will definitely help in your journey.

The guide is available at
www.BrodieEDU.com/resources

About the Author

Paul Brodie is the President of BrodieEDU, an education consulting firm that specializes in the development of literacy programs, motivational seminars for universities and corporations, coaching, and wellness education. Brodie also serves as a Special Education Teacher for the Hurst-Euless-Bedford Independent School District.

From 2011-2014, Brodie served as a Grant

Coordinator for the ASPIRE program in the Birdville Independent School District. As coordinator, he created instructional and enrichment programming for over 800 students and 100 parents in the ASPIRE before and after school programs. He also served for many years on the Board of Directors for the Leadership Development Council, Inc. with leading the implementation of educational programming in low cost housing.

Previously, Brodie spent many years in the corporate world and decided to leave a lucrative career in the medical field to follow his passion and transitioned into education. From 2008 to 2011, he was a highly successful teacher in Arlington, TX where he taught English as a Second Language. Brodie turned a once struggling ESL program into one of the top programs in the school district. Many of his students have moved on to journalism, AVID, art classes, and a number of the students exited the ESL program entirely. His methods included music, movies, graphic novels, and many high engagement methods including using technology, games, cultural celebrations, and getting parents involved in their children's education. Brodie's approach has been called unconventional but highly effective, revolutionary, and highly engaging.

Brodie earned an M.A. in Teaching from Louisiana College and B.B.A. in Management from the University of Texas at Arlington. Brodie is a bestselling author and has written four books. He wrote his first book, Eat Less and Move More: My Journey in the summer of 2015. Brodie's goal of the book was to help those like himself who have had challenges with weight. The goal of his first book was to promote not only weight loss but also health and wellness. He is also the author of Motivation 101 and Positivity Attracts. All three books are Amazon bestsellers and are based on his motivational seminars and struggles with weight. His fourth book, Book Publishing for Beginners was published in January 2016 and has already helped many people realize their dream of becoming a successful published author.

His motivational seminars have been featured at multiple universities and at leadership conferences across the United States since 2005. Brodie is active in professional organizations and within the community and currently serves on the Advisory Board for Advent Urban Youth Development and as a volunteer with the Special Olympics. He continues to be involved with The International Business Fraternity of Delta Sigma Pi and has served in many positions since 2002 including National Vice President –

Organizational Development, Leadership Foundation Trustee, National Organizational Development Chair, District Director, and in many other volunteer leadership roles. He resides in Arlington, TX.

Acknowledgments

Thank you to God for guidance and protection throughout my life.

Thank YOU the reader for investing your time reading this book.

Thank you to my amazing mom, Barbara Brodie for all of the years of support and a kick in the butt when needed.

Thank you to my awesome sister, Dr. Heather Ottaway for all of the help and feedback with my books and also with my motivational seminars. It is scary how similar we are.

Thank you to my best friend, J. Dean Craig for writing the foreword for this book. It meant a lot to me that you were able to take the time to write such an outstanding foreword.

Thank you to Devin Hacker for serving as the editor of my fifth book. The slicing and dicing was very much appreciated and I could not have gotten this book published without her assistance.

Thank you to Lindsay Palmer who is working tirelessly to get me booked on college campuses for seminars throughout the United States. I could not have a better team of people to work with on Team Brodie.

Thank you to all who have served on the BrodieEDU Advisory Board.

Thank you to my dad, Bill "The Wild Scotsman" Brodie for his encouragement and support with the startup process of my books.

Thank you to Shannon and Robert Winckel (two members of the four horsemen with myself and our good friend, Derrada Rubell-Asbell) for their friendship and support. Shannon and Robert are two of my best teacher friends and are always great sounding boards for ideas.

Thank you to (Don) Omar Sandoval for his friendship and help with several BrodieEDU projects including building our awesome website.

Thank you to all of the amazing friends that I have worked with over the past twenty plus years. Each of them has made a great impact on my life.

Thank you to all of my students that I have had the honor to teach over the years. I am very proud of each of my kids.

Thank you to Delta Sigma Pi Business Fraternity. I learned a great deal about public speaking and leadership through the organization and every experience that I have had helped me become the person that I am today.

Thank you to my three best friends: J. Dean Craig, Jen Moorman, and Aaron Krzycki. We have gone through a lot together and I look forward to many more years of friendship.

Thank you to all of the students past and present at the UT Arlington and UT Austin chapters of DSP. Both schools mean a lot to me and I look forward to seeing them again at some point in the near future.

Thank you to the Lott Family (Stacy, Kerry, Lexi, and Austin) for their friendship over the past six years.

Thank you to Robin Clites for always taking care of things at the house with ensuring that Mom and I can always get that family vacation every year.

Contact Information

Interested in booking Paul for seminars, coaching, or consulting?

Paul can be reached at Brodie@BrodieEDU.com

Website www.BrodieEDU.com

Check out all of Paul's books at www.brodieedu.com/books/

Testimonials from Paul's seminar attendees

@BrodieEDU on Twitter

Paul G. Brodie author page on Facebook

Paul G. Brodie author page on Amazon

BrodieEDU Facebook Page

BrodieEDU YouTube Channel

Feedback

Please leave a review for my book as I would greatly appreciate your feedback.

I also welcome you to contact me with any suggestions at Brodie@BrodieEDU.com

Made in the USA
Middletown, DE
09 December 2017